Lean Enterprise

*The Essential Step-by-Step
Guide to Building a Lean Business
with Six Sigma, Kanban, and 5S
Methodologies*

purposes only and are the owned by the owners themselves, not affiliated with this document.

Table of Contents

Part One: The Principles Behind Lean Thinking **6**

Introduction: What Do We Mean By "Lean Enterprise"? 7

Chapter 1: How Lean Businesses Are Built 19

Chapter 2: The Primary Wastes Of Lean Systems 36

Chapter 3: The Major Benefits Of Going Lean 53

Part Two: Tools For Building Lean Systems **65**

Chapter 4: The (Lean) Six Sigma Methodology For Continuous Improvement 66

Chapter 5: The Kanban System For Backlog Reduction 78

Chapter 6: The 5s Process For Workspace
Organization 85

**Conclusion: Greatness Is Possible In The
Absence Of Wastes...............................93**

Thank You 99

Resources Page 100

PART ONE

The Principles Behind Lean Thinking

"Improvement usually means doing something that we have never done before."

—Shigeo Shingo

Introduction:

What Do We Mean by "Lean Enterprise"?

"The difference between market takers and market makers isn't product innovation, it's business model innovation."

—Vala Afshar

What sets apart the companies that have stood the test of time from those that failed to take off? Well, aside from learning how to polish their branding, they continuously work on improving their human capital and management systems — changing accordingly with the times, and adjusting their strategies as they seem fit.

In contrast, brands that were never heard of again weren't able to plant a firm footing in the industry. It's mainly because each step in their workflow had issues that they weren't able to solve. It most likely didn't occur all at once, though. More often than not, a failed business' downfall started with a seemingly harmless misstep — until the rest of their system followed.

No matter how seemingly good a product or a service may be, it will only remain relevant to the market that it's supposed to serve if the whole work process is meticulously addressed. This is especially necessary during the beginning phases of building a business. The

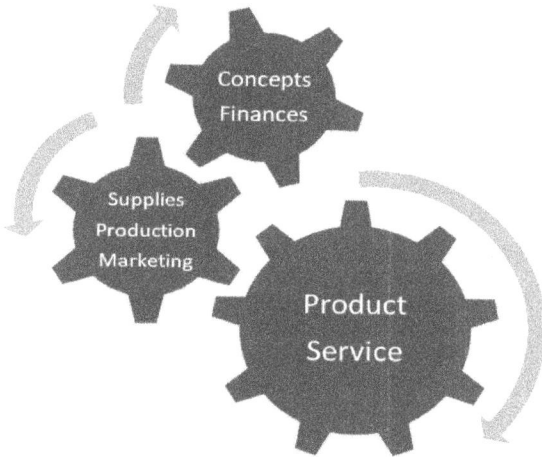

key is to lay down everything such that they will move in sync, so that when one part starts working, the rest will simply go with the right flow

Figure 1. *Simplified analogy of the relationships between work processes and a company's desired output*

The supposed workflow of any organization can be compared to a group of gears working in unison to move an entire machine. Figure 1 is just an ultra-simplified version of how products and services — or more generally, outputs — are related to all the steps that come before it. So long as the gears are constantly well-oiled and nothing gets caught in them, the machine will move and operate as it should.

However, when faulty components start slowing down the movement of the smaller cogwheels, every part of the process becomes inefficient. Ultimately, the biggest cogwheel will be affected, and no output will be delivered according to the company's set standards — if any had been set at all.

This is why all parts of a process must be constantly assessed and measured. Otherwise, improvement will almost always be impossible, and moving towards the next goals will just remain a pipedream.

Thus, if you don't get your act together within the company, you're bound to offer people a bunch of products that aren't serving any real purpose for them. This may also damage your relationships with investors and suppliers. All it takes is another careless mistake and your reputation will now be forever tainted.

Successful businesses are going to have none of that. They know exactly how to get things done by using the most effective processes that they have applied through the years. Otherwise, they wouldn't be able to keep their gears rolling at the speed they want to. The question is, are they going through their workflow in the most cost-efficient and most resourceful way possible?

Lean Company, Lean Manufacturing, and Lean Enterprise

It's one thing to know how to get the job done. It's another thing to know how to get it done outstandingly. But it's a whole other level to know how to deliver high-quality outputs using the least amount of wastes and resources. Given the complexity of planning and production, it's normal to wonder whether it's possible that simple waste elimination can lead to the best products and services.

This is where the concept of lean thinking comes in. At its core, lean thinking focuses on how to come up with better methods of utilizing financial and human capital. Its ultimate goal is to provide maximum benefits not just to loyal and potential customers, but also to society as a whole.

This system attempts to operate on the idea that if each individual or group in the entire system can identify and eliminate the biggest wastes in their tasks, then all of them — as a whole — will be able to produce more valuable outputs using far less expenses. Not only will this drive an organization to its golden age, but it will also develop its employees' overall competence and confidence in themselves.

Lean thinking is the basis for all efficiency-driven mechanisms that are practiced in companies, manufacturing or productions, and even enterprises. But what does it really mean when every aspect of an organization is "lean"?

The following items illustrate the general idea of how lean enterprises are built:

- **Step 1: Building a Lean Company**

This is a company that follows lean thinking methodologies when it comes to production. Each step of the process has been aligned with the rest of the workflow to give way to a smooth and continuous cycle. Goals are typically addressed by creating a team that is composed of experts from various departments (cross-functional team).

- **Step 2: Employing Lean Manufacturing**

Also called "lean production", this involves a series of systematic methods for eliminating wastes and hurdles within production processes. It carefully assesses the wastes caused by uneven workloads, evens them out, and minimizes the chances of overburdening staff to improve output value and overall costs. A lean company abides by a number of lean manufacturing principles to enhance the workflow — beginning from the conceptualization phase, distribution, and even beyond.

- **Step 3: Establishing a Lean Enterprise**

This can be regarded as the ultimate product of all the offshoots of lean thinking. The lean enterprise is a grand collaboration among a number of companies — all of which are working to perfect a product or service that all of them will benefit from. The caveat, however, is that it can be tough for a lean company to reach its full potential if it's working with companies that aren't following lean methodologies.

Lean Thinking and Lean Behaviors

For lean thinking to make it to the enterprise level, it needs to be perfected on a personal level first. If individuals can make their tasks more efficient, these seemingly minute improvements are bound to translate to enterprise-wide successes.

However, members must also learn how to trade extreme individualism for team effort. It is inevitable that certain members or teams may have legitimate needs that are in conflict with other components of the system. A strong sense of cooperation then becomes necessary, which can only be achieved when all individuals agree to expand their roles in the name of a company or an enterprise's ultimate goal.

Members of cross-functional teams are usually trained to become more well-rounded. For example, full allegiance to their original function (e.g. marketing, financing, engineering, design, production) isn't encouraged in a lean environment. Team-oriented thinking and behaviors are needed to ensure that no phase in the workflow will ever end up being stuck.

This is why it's necessary for members of cross-

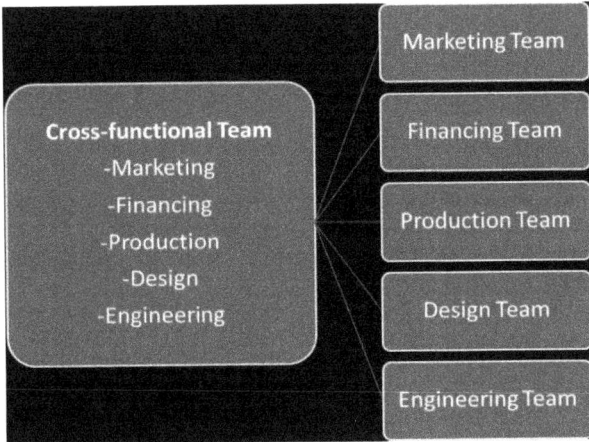

functional teams to accept, right from the beginning, that they will need to pursue an offshoot of their original career path to succeed as an employee of a lean company. Instead of performing their original function, they now work together with other experts to establish new value-adding processes or best practices for the roles that people like them play in an organization.

Figure 2. *Individuals from specialized backgrounds form a cross-functional team to* *develop better processes for the teams that perform the tasks involved in the workflow*

Figure 2 illustrates how the members of a cross-functional team work with each other to develop a grand system that will sync team roles for maximum efficiency. They will look into the various roadblocks that get caught up between tasks performed by different teams. Once they come up with a viable solution, they will then meet with the respective teams so they can start implementing the new and improved system.

Now, when these roles are translated to the lean enterprise, member companies will need to establish new behavioral standards that will help regulate behaviors and activities involved in the enterprise workflow. What's important is that companies focus on what they're really good at to become a reliable member of the enterprise.

Lean as the Key to Productivity

In order for a lean enterprise to succeed, member companies need to refine their existing models to become more adept at doing more tasks using less resources. The problem is, while companies work towards eliminating wastes in their processes, this may cause stress in their employees, who fear that they might eventually be laid off from their jobs due to redundancy. Hence, companies need to explore and exhaust all of their options when it comes to job preservation as they work towards becoming lean.

Becoming a lean company may take years before you notice the fruits of all your efforts. Of course, when you have more wastes to eliminate, you also need more time to straighten out your workflow. This book will give you an overview of what you need to go through, plus the tools that can help you accomplish this huge task.

The lean models of business may be the key to building a company — and eventually an enterprise — that will generate the workflow efficiency that you've always wanted. If you're looking for ways to improve how business is done within your company, gradually shifting to lean thinking will not only help you increase your overall productivity, but also provide your employees with their much-needed career growth.

Chapter 1:

How Lean Businesses are Built

"Every job is a self-portrait of the person who did it.

Autograph your work with excellence."

—Jessica Guidobono

In order to understand how to build a lean enterprise, it's important to learn how lean businesses are built first. Lean thinking within a company is often considered the foundation of pursuing lean practices, no matter what level you may be at. After all, it would be difficult to translate certain practices to bigger scales if you can't make it work at the lowest levels.

Lean thinking is known to enhance your workflow's speed and agility. Generally, it helps you become adaptable and competent enough to continue providing customer value in a world where people's needs are constantly changing.

19

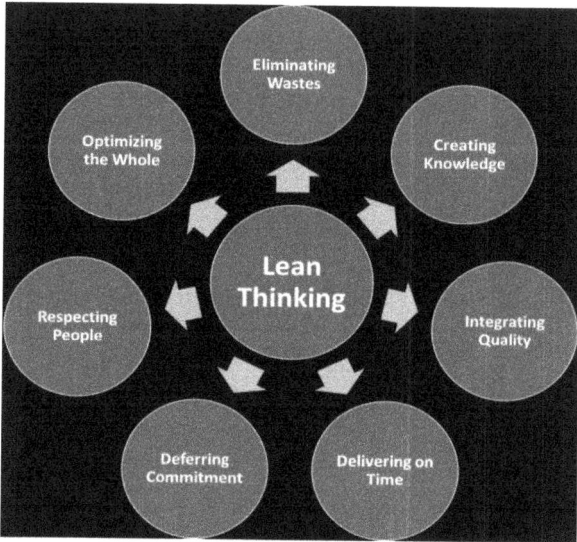

The 7 Principles of Lean Thinking

Figure 3. *A general illustration of how lean thinking works*

Lean thinking primarily started as a required practice in Toyota's manufacturing floor. The term "lean thinking" was first coined by James Womack and Daniel Jones in their book, *Lean*

Thinking: Banish Waste and Create Wealth in Your Corporation.

All of their insights were a result of their comprehensive study of the Toyota Production System (TPS). They noticed that Toyota focused on creating system frameworks that makes manufacturing a lot more value-adding and efficient. Most lean strategies that you'll come across can be traced back to the wide success of the TPS. It remains the primary reference where most lean manufacturing methods are based.

Any business that is trying to get into the lean mindset will need to integrate the following principles into their processes:

- **Eliminating Wastes**

Wastes found within the knowledge workflow are usually linked to the management and to the people doing the work, and not exactly on the production floor. Examples of wastes involved in the knowledge work are:

- Context Switching: This occurs when people need to switch from one tool or platform to the other just to complete a single task. This may involve opening a ton of programs or apps all at once.

It usually requires a certain order to accomplish so it's prone to confusion. In a way, it overlaps with multitasking since your attention is scattered across various tasks.

-        Poor Appropriation of Tools: Sometimes, slow completion time can mainly be blamed on inappropriate tools. Oftentimes, when employees are forced to use a tool that certainly isn't the best for the job, the production flow doesn't move as quickly as it should.

-        Inefficiency of Information Systems: This is related to the previous point. If the workflow relies heavily on information systems, yet company reports say that these systems aren't helping like they're supposed to, you can't expect that things will be accomplished as planned.

It's even worse when user feedback isn't integrated into the design — either before the system was launched or after a system overhaul had been made.

- <u>Ineffective Communication Among Teams:</u> The phrase "communication is key" isn't emphasized in many contexts for nothing. The lack of open communication and transparency is often the cause of many delays during the production process.

- <u>Lack of Viable Market:</u> Any factor in your product that your customer wouldn't be willing to pay for is ultimately considered a waste in the whole workflow. What's the use of something if nobody wants it?

• **Creating Knowledge**

For companies to become a truly lean business, knowledge and learning must be integrated into the organization. When employees are constantly given the chance to learn the industry's best practices from experts, not only can they add more value to the work they do, but they also learn how to be valuable in other ways. This is typically done by:

- Having retrospectives

- Cross-training employees

-      Holding   regular   discussions   about employees' work processes

When a company values knowledge creation, they will be able to perform their tasks with more value at a much faster rate. This is a way for them to constantly update their skills and competencies.

• **Integrating Quality**

A company that envisions long-term growth needs to utilize systems that are as error-free as possible. Lean companies usually do this by automating tasks that are repetitive, mentally uninteresting, and prone to human error.

As a result, employees can pour their time and focus on skills that actually engage them mentally. This allows them to devote themselves fully to the pursuit of both personal and company growth.

• **Delivering on Time**

Lean thinking is primarily driven by the idea that focus is the root of all high-quality outputs. When your work environment isn't conducive enough to maintain an uncluttered mind, this slows your work down. Top-quality work is hard to produce when an employee is constantly distracted.

Lean systems always have steady workflows. This means that everything is delivered and accomplished on a consistent, predictable basis. A bad workflow, on the other hand, is always unpredictable because of unsustainable and unreliable work habits.

Lean teams are always refining their workflows to optimize value at every level. They do this by greatly limiting their WIPs (works in progress) and providing a good work environment so nothing gets stuck in the workload traffic. Multitasking is prohibited because it only prevents people from finishing tasks on time.

- **Deferring Commitment**

Careful planning is necessary to accomplish long-term goals. In lean thinking, however, it is discouraged to plan for a product's release way out in advance. This prevents having stocks that may only end up being useless.

Instead, it recommends that you decide to pursue something at the last responsible moment — during the time when you've thoroughly considered all the factors that would help you come up with the best decision possible.

This goes back to the main goal of all lean systems: eliminating wastes.

Deferring commitment helps you decide more smartly by going over the data and reports that accurately reflect the current market situation. This prevents you from pursuing seemingly innovative projects that don't really translate into an urgent or even viable market need in reality.

• **Respecting People**

The root of a lean system's success all boils down to one basic thing: respect.

First, the concept of lean was born out of a desire to respect the customer's needs and preferences. Second, lean systems are able to thrive because their employees are well-respected by their superiors. They are provided with environments that encourage them to perform at their best.

On an individual level, respect generally entails maintaining kindness and courtesy to everyone that you're working with — whether it's your superiors, your colleagues, your employees, or your customers. Respect is also often shown through:

- Providing safe environments for idea sharing

- Encouraging employees to develop themselves in whatever way they wish

- Trusting employees' decision-making processes

Respect goes a long way in lean systems because trust is required to maintain good workflow. After all, building good relationships is the key to creating a stable system that produces high-value outputs.

- **Optimizing the Whole Organization**

All decisions in a lean company must be made relative to the whole organization. For instance, decisions to optimize processes must not only involve one team — it must involve everybody else.

Naturally, an improvement in one component can already be enough to see significant differences in the workflow. However, to become truly lean means to address all possible sources of waste.

Building a lean enterprise all starts with creating a lean business. The next step would be to find others who also share the same lean ideas as you do. Maintaining collaborations among companies can already be difficult enough since each member will have their own goals and agendas. However, if all of you can work towards operating under the same lean system, then overall work and production is going to be a breeze.

The 5 Principles of Lean Manufacturing

Many businesses are beginning to switch to lean thinking and lean manufacturing to develop the kinds of products that have a good chance of penetrating the global market. Aside from consistently meeting customer demands, it also enables them to earn more profits and enhance product quality with less cost.

Lean thinking gave way to the five lean

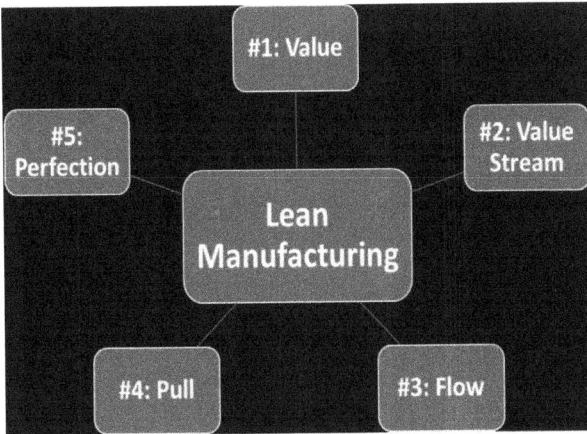

manufacturing principles that have greatly improved the workflow of many successful companies today. These are often considered

as key factors in improving overall efficiency in the workplace.

Figure 4. *How lean manufacturing moves from one phase to the next*

- **Defining Value**

The first step of lean manufacturing begins with learning what exactly the customer values in a particular product or service. This will help a business determine how much a customer is willing to pay for what, which then allows them to set a reasonable target price. After which, the cost of manufacturing the product will then be defined.

To properly establish value in a lean system, it is vital to learn about the market's recognized and latent needs.

While some customers may already know what they want exactly, others may not be aware that there might be a product or service out there that they actually want or need. Or perhaps, they know they need a particular something, but cannot express what it's supposed to be.

That's where market research comes in. This is typically done through interviews, demographic assessment, web analytics, user testing, surveys, etc.

By defining what your customers really want, you get to create something of great value — not just a product that seems innovative in theory. This also helps you understand your customers' purchasing power, as well as the way in which they want this product to be delivered to them.

• Determining and Planning the Value Stream

The value stream consists of all the activities that allow you to conceptualize and create the most useful yet most profitable product that matches the customer values that have been defined in the first step.

This is the product's journey from the raw materials stage all the way to the customer usage stage. The stream even includes the customer's eventual disposal of the product, which paves the way for considerable upgrades in the next release.

Naturally, activities that do not provide value at the end of the value stream (customer) are regarded as wastes. These wastes can be subdivided into two types: necessary waste (e.g. quality control) and pure waste (e.g. supplier delays).

The latter should be completely eliminated, while the former should be continuously perfected so they don't get in the way of the value stream. Otherwise, they'd only delay the rest of the process.

• **Creating Flow**

A river will always make its way to the ocean eventually, provided that nothing stops the water in its tracks. However, a significant amount of debris in one part of the river system may cause the water to be trapped and unable to follow its natural path.

This is exactly what waste does in a value stream. It interrupts the natural flow of the production process, causing delays that might start out small. Eventually, however, it might end up becoming a massive setback that prevents everything from moving further forward.

That said, a company must take their time to fully understand their flow systems to eliminate wastes effectively and completely. The concept of flow in lean manufacturing is all about creating a series of steps that are in sync with each other — one that hardly ever gets interrupted.

- **Setting Pull**

One of the most significant wastes involved in manufacturing is inventory. To solve this, a pull-based system must be established. This system aims to minimize inventories and works in progress as much as possible. Relevant materials should always be available to maintain the company's flow.

Instead of creating products way ahead of schedule based only on market forecasts, a pull-based system encourages you to begin working on something only when a customer expresses the need for it. Thus, you'll only begin production at the moment of need, and only in the quantities requested.

This allows you to develop the most efficient way to assemble a product, as you need to deliver your promise within a reasonable timeframe.

• **Pursuing Perfection**

The first four principles of lean manufacturing are all about identifying and reducing wastes as much as possible. This last principle is the crucial point that holds all lean thinking concepts together. Perfection based on company standards helps deliver products in the best state possible to the end user.

Although a perfect product can never technically exist, pursuing perfection is what inspires companies to continue serving their customers to the best of their abilities.

This is what ultimately sets them apart from the competition. After all, if small mistakes can be removed from the value stream every single day, there will come a time when errors will be close to non-existent.

The shift towards lean thinking may not exactly be an easy task, especially if you've just realized that you have major roadblocks in all the steps of your value stream. But when you've identified what exactly your problem areas are, you've already taken the first step in creating a more efficient business. Applying the principles of lean thinking and lean manufacturing gives you a more competitive edge, simply because you've addressed all of your wastes.

Takeaway:

•   Lean thinking becomes possible when an organization consistently works on waste elimination, knowledge creation, quality integration, timely deliveries, smart commitments, respect, and overall process optimization.

•   Lean manufacturing helps you focus on what truly creates value for your customer. By eliminating all the pure wastes in the value stream, you can create a smooth and steady flow that will allow you to pursue perfection.

Chapter 2:

The Primary Wastes of Lean Systems

"If you define the problem correctly, you almost have the solution."

—Steve Jobs

Every industry abides by their own sets of best practices. Lean thinking practices, on the other hand, seem to be valuable in every type of business context. After all, it does get rid of significant setbacks that prevent processes from properly moving forward.

But how exactly do lean systems eliminate their wastes and problems? How does it ensure that every person within the value stream are working only as necessary, and using components only in the needed amounts? How is it able to maintain that kind of focus as the tasks flow down the value stream?

The Toyota Production System (TPS)

In Chapter 1, we mentioned in passing that the Toyota Production System (TPS) is the precursor of all lean manufacturing methods. In this section, we will further elaborate on the concepts that have turned the TPS into a timeless lean thinking reference — something that has been extremely useful for many businesses today.

Just-in-Time (JIT) and Jidoka

The overall success of the TPS stands on two conceptual pillars: just-in-time and jidoka. This approach was created by Taiichi Ohno, an industrial engineer who is considered the father of TPS. It aimed to solve 3 key issues that are often encountered in the value stream: inconsistency (muri), overburden (mura), and waste (muda). Improvements in the production line are usually achieved by:

• Eliminating inconsistency in the value stream by automating repetitive tasks, thereby smoothening the flow all the way down to the final output.

• Minimizing overburdens or company-wide stress as a result of removing inconsistencies (i.e. far less errors flowing into the value stream).

• Improving stress levels among employees and managers, which significantly reduces the wastes that have to be cleaned up later on.

The just-in-time thinking operates on the principle that businesses should produce only the parts and outputs that they need, only on the moment that they need it, and only in the quantities that they need. Hence, even when products aren't assembled ahead of time, a lean business will still be able to put it all together in a timely, "just-in-time" manner. This is usually how the process goes:

• Upon receiving an order, the first phase of the production line is prompted to start the production process.

• There must be enough stocks of all the needed parts in the assembly line. It must be no more or no less than what has actually been ordered. This ensures that the product can be put together as efficiently as possible.

•   All the parts that have been used in assembling one product are replaced. Only the same number of parts should be retrieved to prevent overstocking.

•   As for manufactured parts, the production line must only make the particular

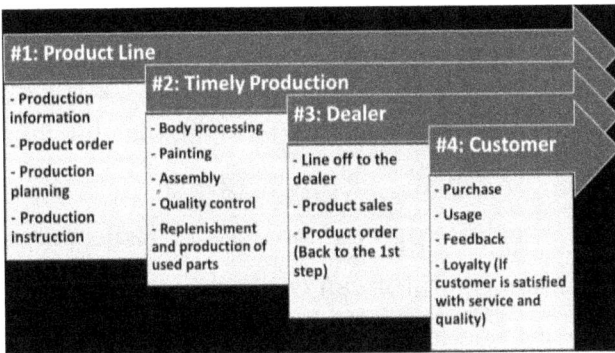

#1: Product Line	#2: Timely Production	#3: Dealer	#4: Customer
- Production information - Product order - Production planning - Production instruction	- Body processing - Painting - Assembly - Quality control - Replenishment and production of used parts	- Line off to the dealer - Product sales - Product order (Back to the 1st step)	- Purchase - Usage - Feedback - Loyalty (If customer is satisfied with service and quality)

•   parts that have been retrieved. This makes them prepared for the next production cycle once a product has been ordered again.

Figure 5. *A simplified chart of how just-in-time and jidoka play out in Toyota*

To ensure that the JIT system moves smoothly, quality control must be applied. This is achieved with the help of jidoka, which means "automation with a human touch". It involves a machine that stops on its own once the normal production cycle is completed, or when it detects a defect in a product. This reduces wastes or "muda", since it prevents the production from creating more defective items.

Only those that have passed quality control will be able to proceed to the next steps in the value stream. Since a particular machine automatically stops as soon as an issue arises, the human operator can continue working using another functional machine. Then, they can assess the root cause of the first machine's problem.

A single human operator can manage multiple machines, increasing the company's overall productivity. This doesn't only make it easier to identify problems, but it also minimizes delays by allowing the workflow to proceed as planned.

DOWNTIME: The 8 Deadly Wastes of Lean Systems

Manufacturing wastes come in various forms. We already know in theory that the lean manufacturing framework is all about keeping your value stream and final products aligned by minimizing wastes. But what are wastes, exactly? How do they play out in the real world?

So far, the TPS has identified 8 deadly wastes of lean systems. This can be easily remembered by the acronym DOWNTIME, which stands for:

- **Defects**

- **Overproduction**

- **Waiting**

- **Non-utilized Talent**

- **Transportation**

- **Inventory**

- **Motion**

- **Excess Processing**

1. *Defects*

A defect refers to any mistake that needs additional effort, money, resources, or time to rectify. In non-lean productions, defects

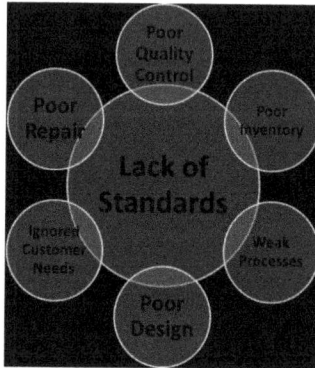

typically halt the flow of the value stream because of a component that needs to be completely remade.

Figure 6. *The lack of standards is usually the root cause of all manufacturing defects*

The truth is, all wastes can never be fully eliminated. However, if you can work on eliminating defects, the rest of the lean wastes will follow suit. This can usually be accomplished by standardizing all aspects of the production process and applying stricter quality controls at every point of the value stream.

2. *Overproduction*

This is often the result of not following the pull-based or JIT-jidoka systems. As we have learned, lean systems try to minimize wastes by producing and assembling parts only when they are needed. Overproduction can get the value stream stuck when the flow ends up in a bottleneck. This is generally caused by:

• Just-in-case production as opposed to just-in-time production

• Producing based on uninformed forecasts

• Changes in product design and engineering

• Long production and assembly times

• Unassessed customer needs

• Ineffective automation processes

To solve issues with overproduction, it's important to focus on what the customer really cares about, and then develop the most straightforward value stream. This ensures that none of the company's efforts will ever be put to waste.

3.   *Waiting*

This happens when there's been a hold-up somewhere in the value stream. For instance, everything may have to be stopped because of machine breakdowns, lack of complete supplies, lack of approval from higher-ups, or overwhelmed staff. All of these may happen due to:

• Insufficient or unreliable staff (and managers)

• Staff absences

• Uneven workloads

• Unexpected downtimes

• Poor communication and processing

Just like overproduction, this waste is typically due to process bottlenecks. One way of solving this is by having enough staff so that the workload is evenly distributed at these points.

Although you may think that having a smaller staff can help you save money from salaries, it may actually incur even more expenses. This is because waiting and delays cost more money than simply paying a few more people to do the job well.

4.   *Non-utilized Talent*

This wasn't part of the TPS' original list of lean wastes, but this has become quite a common occurrence in many modern businesses. This happens when a company fails to utilize their staff in the best way possible. This is often seen through:

• Poor communication among departments

• Poor management

• Insufficient staff training

• Lack of cooperation

• Inefficient workflow at the admin level

• Mismatch between an employee's skills and their given tasks

Improper utilization of staff's skills and talents may not seem like a big deal, but its bad effects over the long-term is usually made apparent

45

when the whole company fails to reach its goals within their scheduled timeframes. It's also one of the main reasons why there is a resounding lack of employee engagement within a company. On the other hand, businesses usually thrive once they begin to give employees the recognition that they deserve.

5. *Transportation*

This doesn't only refer to actual transportation by a vehicle from one place to the next. Transportation is a general term that covers any process that involves getting something from Point A to Point B — even if the task is purely digital in nature. For instance, sending memos via e-mail can already be considered as "transport". Oftentimes, transportation wastes are results of:

- Wasteful steps in the value stream

- Workflow that is out of sync

- Poorly-designed processes and systems

- Bad office layouts and/or poor planning of office locations

The longer it takes for a product to get where it's supposed to, the higher the transportation costs will be. Not only does this waste time, but it also makes the product more prone to deterioration and damage. Transportation wastes can be eliminated by simplifying workflows, improving layouts, or simply shortening the physical distances between steps.

6. *Inventory*

More often than not, inventories are necessities for a business — especially for one that is highly in demand. Production lines will need raw materials and manufactured parts that are value-adding to the final product.

The retrieval processes for these materials need to be well-documented in order to spot any errors more conveniently. Additionally, having enough stock will allow you to be more adaptable when it comes to following through with the customer's needs.

The thing is, inventory can sometimes be the

source of problems in lean systems. This is usually illustrated using the ship metaphor.

Figure 7. *How inventory hides a ton of company problems*

As Figure 7 shows, your company moves as a ship in an ocean called "inventory". As long as the ocean you're moving in is at a safe water level, your ship will be able to go to wherever it wishes. However, what you don't know is that there are problems lurking beneath the surface — as represented by the rocks.

Just because you're able to move as usual, it doesn't mean that problems aren't there. In fact,

48

it may only take a slight shift in water level before your ship finally hits one of those rocks. Examples of issues that are hidden by inventory are:

- Poor documentation and management

- Incompetent monitoring systems

- Unclear communication

- Lack of foresight

- Defective deliveries

- Unreliable suppliers

- Inconsistent manufacturing speeds

- Untrained or mismatched staff

Still going by the metaphor, this means that you need to dive deep into your inventories to figure out whether rocks are just waiting for their turn to bust through your ship. Once these issues have been detected, you must do whatever it takes to eliminate those rocks so you can steer your ship in any direction — without worrying about the water level.

7. *Motion*

Wastes relating to motion are quite similar to transportation wastes. This involves non-value adding steps that are covered by machines or employees. In contrast with transportation wastes, motion wastes are found in any unnecessary movement within the value stream. Generally, motion is affected by:

• Bad workstation or shop layouts

• Badly designed processes

• Bottleneck in workstations caused by shared tools

• Poor staff training

Eliminating motion wastes can be as simple as making the movement between workstations more convenient. More often than not, the reason why people aren't driven to do what they have to do is because the layout and circumstances make doing the task utterly inconvenient and difficult.

8. *Excess Processing*

While lean systems are all about providing quality, sometimes even quality controls can be over the top. Customers will only need a few key things, and constantly checking for something that goes beyond that only adds to waste. That's because you're investing time and resources in certain things when the customers have zero interest in what you're trying to offer.

Quality controls are necessary but only if they actually help in the value stream. All attempts at quality control must be designed to serve only what the customer considers important. You may have good intentions with your unsolicited updates, but unless the customer wants it, that will largely just go unappreciated.

In order for your business to go lean, you must first discover the factors that produce the most wastes in your current value stream. You can't just shift to a new system without knowing what's wrong with the current one in the first place.

Once these problems have been identified, it then becomes so much easier to conceptualize solutions that can eliminate them completely. Then, when every part of the process is free of waste, you'd soon be able to see that your company had that much potential all along.

Takeaway:

• The Toyota Production System started out as a practice for eliminating 3 key issues in the production line: inconsistency (muri), overburden (mura), and waste (muda). It is the main precursor of all the lean thinking and manufacturing systems that we know of today.

• DOWNTIME is the main roadblock of all lean systems. Getting rid of the waste from these components gives your work processes a lot more room to flow to where it should go.

Chapter 3:

The Major Benefits of Going Lean

"The product that wins is the one that bridges customers to the future,

not the one that requires a giant leap."

—Aaron Levie

Becoming lean as an individual can make a big difference in your tasks as an employee. When you apply its concepts consistently enough, they're bound to affect your life's other aspects positively. Over time, you'll find that you're able to process decisions in a more systematic way. If lean concepts can have such a profound effect on a personal level, you can just imagine the possibilities if you scale the leanness all the way to an enterprise.

Shifting to Lean: What's in It for You?

Lean thinking encourages people to apply doable changes in small increments. The ultimate goal is to speed up all the workflows within a system without compromising product or service quality. Lean is certainly not a quick fix for eliminating company wastes. It involves being in a long-term commitment with continuous growth and improvement.

Even if a particular lean technique has been proven effective by many companies, changes certainly didn't happen within a few months of applying the methods. It usually takes far longer than that for anything significant to be noticeable. Of course, it's also understandable how people may feel discouraged to stick with the new methods if the benefits aren't that obvious. To help you stay lean when you're tempted to think that it doesn't work, here's a list of its short-term to long-term benefits:

Short-term Benefits

• Improved Management: Even though problems will still come up every now and then, lean makes the work environment more convenient to deal with if you're a manager. With better task standards in place, it will be easier for you to pinpoint anything that's disrupting the flow of the value stream. Most of the time, you will be able to figure out that something isn't quite right just by looking at an area's set-up or layout.

• <u>Improved Efficiency and Productivity:</u> As a result of standardizing every piece of the workflow, it becomes automatic for employees to know what exactly they need to do — and when they need to do it. It reduces a lot of redundancy and overlaps that stem from task confusion. It also ensures that they are doing their work correctly every single time.

They no longer have to constantly ask whether a particular task is under their responsibility. They can just focus on their own task list without worrying about anything else.

• <u>Safer and More Convenient Layouts:</u> Since literal wastes will be decluttered, turning lean gives your company more space to move around. This will instantly make task movements a lot more convenient. Additionally, it will provide your staff a safer space for working when the layout is reorganized to eliminate hazards.

• <u>Involvement from the Whole Company:</u> Lean is something that isn't applied only to one team or department. When a company decides to go lean, every level of the hierarchy is involved — from those on the top all the way to the ones on the bottom. After all, lean systems depend on the cooperation of everyone involved.

Medium and Long-term Benefits

• <u>Improved Cash Flow:</u> Once you get rid of **DOWNTIME**, you can now focus your energy on ensuring that the value-adding steps of your value stream flows as smoothly as possible. In the absence of roadblocks, workflow bottlenecks, and delays, not only will you be able to deliver products in a just-in-time manner, but you'll also improve the cash flow within your company.

- <u>Customer Satisfaction and Loyalty:</u> Customer satisfaction is one of the most immediate results of applying lean, so they become more likely to trust your brand again in the future. If you keep on doing what works, you're bound to gain their loyalty in the long run.

- <u>Employee Satisfaction and Loyalty:</u> While lean systems are mainly focused on the desires of the customer, it also promotes better mood and morale among employees. The changes may be met with resistance at first, but once they see that it takes them far less time to complete tasks compared to before, they'll become more open to the overall idea of lean.

Additionally, since lean is all about constant improvement and collaborations, they tend to feel better about themselves because they're part of a team that actually cares about others. Lean systems give them a safe space to voice out their concerns and provide suggestions for further improvement.

- **Marketability for Collaboration:** What makes something marketable? In terms of companies, marketable companies are usually the unproblematic ones. You need to be *that* company if you wish to be a part of a lean enterprise. After all, lean is all about efficiency, and you need to be an efficient team player to ensure that you don't disrupt the flow of the entire system.

Lean is not merely an exercise in cost-cutting. It is more of a long-term opportunity for

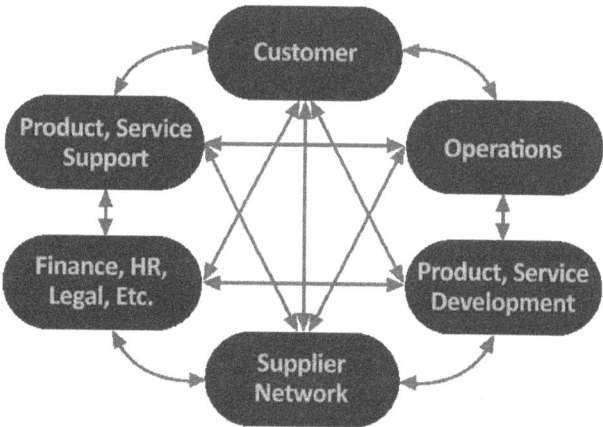

consistent growth. Once you have smoothed out your lean processes within the company, you will eventually become the preferred suppliers of particular products and services.

That's because your consistency and standards translate well to your products — something that lets both customers and collaborators know that you're a company that they can trust. What are the Challenges?

Figure 8. *Various relationships within a lean enterprise*

Lean thinking all sounds good in theory, and it can be exciting to continue applying it once you've seen how great it can be in practice. However, as Figure 8 shows, the tasks between teams or entities cannot always be as conveniently executed as getting from Point A to Point B in a clean, straight line. Their involvement with each other goes back and forth, which emphasizes how every component must be free of wastes to ensure a smooth flow.

Of course, shifting to lean has its own set of issues and challenges. Like any other form of change, you should resist hoping that it would do its "magic" in just a few weeks or months.

Technically speaking, when every factor is ironed out right from the beginning, it can be possible to have everything sorted out in just a short time. But that only applies when the scenario is ideal. Experience will tell you that situations are rarely ever ideal, especially when transitions are concerned.

Here are some issues that you might have to deal with on your way to lean:

- **Cultural Resistance**

This may be the biggest hurdle that you have to get through when transitioning from wasteful to lean. When a status quo has already been set, most people are resistant to any change in the company culture. That's usually a result of staying in their comfort zones for long enough. They feel that change is unnecessary since they already like the current workflow.

To gradually ease the workforce into the lean system, training (or retraining) people must be prioritized. Here's what you need to clarify with them:

- What are the changes that you'll be implementing?

- Why are you implementing them?

\- How are they going to benefit from these changes?

\- How will it benefit the whole company?

Although all four of these are important considerations, they're likely going to be most concerned about the third point, as this involves their role in the company. However, if you can clearly explain the good things about these changes, then people will be more inclined to accept it.

- **Costs and Upkeep**

On a personal level, there are cases in which you'll need to spend money today to be able to profit or save more money in the future.

Going lean requires the same thing. Eliminating wastes will need money, because going for the long-term fix requires money. Eventually, however, the money you spent will eventually go back to you in the form of increased profits from minimized defects.

And, just like your home needs yearly maintenance, lean also requires upkeep. Proper planning and execution will ensure that you won't have to worry about running out of certain parts or having outdated systems.

- **Talent Gaps**

Since lean processes may now require updated technologies, companies that are going lean must bridge the talent gap. This means that they may have to let go of general-labor employees in favor of those who have licenses and certifications to operate lean system equipment. These employees are adept not only at handling these systems, but they are also capable of performing maintenance, inspections, repairs, and designs.

- **Technological Hurdles**

One of the initial costs involved in lean is investing in newer software and technology. Since lean encourages automation in almost every area, it is crucial that you choose the system that doesn't keep you stuck in your old ways. Not all systems are created equal, so you must go through your choices carefully to ensure that you ultimately get the one that is reliable enough to sustain your lean methods.

Implementing lean will not be as straightforward as it seems to be. While lean is there to make processes a lot simpler, going against the usual grain might complicate things at first. This is especially difficult when you already have a set system among your various teams. After all, when you already know how to communicate with other members in a certain way, it does take effort to change all of that into a process that might be the total opposite of what everyone is used to.

The most effective companies and enterprises know how to mobilize the entire workforce to create the best products or services for their customers. Lean thinking can help you do just that, because you'll no longer be caught up in problem-solving all the time. Your focus can now shift towards your company's biggest asset, which are your employees' talents.

Takeaway:

• Lean thinking is beneficial from the personal level all the way up to the enterprise level. The short-term gains typically involve a more efficient and less stressful workflow on a daily basis, while long-term gains are all about multifactorial company growth.

• Shifting to lean can be a challenging endeavor, especially when you're met with all sorts of resistance. The biggest problem, perhaps, is the resistance from your own workforce due to ingrained company culture. Fortunately, it only takes a bit of planning and foresight to get past these hurdles.

PART TWO

Tools for Building Lean Systems

"However beautiful the strategy, you should occasionally look at the results."
—Winston Churchill

Chapter 4:

The (Lean) Six Sigma Methodology for Continuous Improvement

"Continuous improvement is better than delayed perfection."

—Mark Twain

All businesses have components that they can improve on. If you have never thoroughly assessed your processes before, it can indeed be difficult to determine which areas are ripe for improvement. It therefore becomes essential to streamline your workflows first so it's easier to identify where the process bottlenecks are.

Lean, Six Sigma, and Lean Six Sigma

The first part of this book focuses on the most important lean concepts that can transform your business into a more efficient manufacturing machine. In this chapter, we will discuss another tool that seeks to eliminate waste: Six Sigma.

Lean and Six Sigma are waste elimination systems that are both popular in manufacturing. In essence, they share the same end goal of process efficiency — they just have different approaches in getting things done. One of their key differences is their waste identification methods. Lean identifies wastes by examining the company's 8 Deadly Wastes (DOWNTIME). Meanwhile, Six Sigma does this by using the DMAIC (Define, Measure, Analyze, Improve, Control) method.

Lean vs. Six Sigma

Lean primarily focuses on eliminating steps that don't add any value to the final product. Value is regarded as anything that customers appreciate enough to actually pay for. For instance, motion or movement isn't really something that customers would willingly pay for when they get their product. One of the goals of lean is to limit such wastes as much as possible, as they aren't really value-adding.

Six Sigma, on the other hand, relies on data to solve problems within work processes. It puts a heavy emphasis on customer satisfaction by minimizing product defects. At its core, Six Sigma aims for a 99.99996% defect-free rate. You can expect a Six Sigma workflow to only have 3.4 defects or less out of a million outputs. Defects are any factor in the product that doesn't satisfy customer expectations.

As you may notice, both lean and Six Sigma care about what the customer ultimately wants. The focus of their approach is what mainly sets them apart. Lean works toward increasing the flow (or reducing traffic) within the value stream, while Six Sigma chases consistency in their processes and outputs.

Essentially, here's how lean and Six Sigma go about eliminating wastes:

• Lean lowers total production time and limits the use of resources to ultimately maximize customer value.

- Six Sigma aims for product perfection through reduced variation to ultimately reduce costs and improve customer perception.

Lean Six Sigma: Waste Elimination Tools

LEAN

Goals: Waste elimination, lower production time

Method: Lean tools (Just-in-time, jidoka, 5S, kanban, etc.)

Usage: Internal (Flow efficiency, cost reduction)

SIX SIGMA

Goals: Process improvement relative to customer needs

Method: DMAIC and other quality tools

Usage: External (Customer satisfaction)

Lean + Waste Elimination = Six Sigma Quality

Six Sigma + Defect Reduction = Lean Speed

Combined

Here's where it gets exciting. What if both of these systems are combined? What if you use lean principles to make your tasks flow as efficiently as possible, and then use the Six

Sigma system to create processes that are consistent across the board?

This is where Lean Six Sigma comes in. Lean is a system that goes for defect detection, while Six Sigma goes for defect reduction. Combined, Lean Six Sigma brings you defect prevention — a methodology that prioritizes both the product quality and customer satisfaction by reducing wastes, production cycles, and product variations, all while standardizing work processes and flow.

Figure 10. *How lean and Six Sigma complement each other*

In a nutshell, Lean Six Sigma is a system that not only improves flow and efficiency, but also enhances the quality of the whole process. As shown in Figure 10, lean and Six Sigma are two similar approaches that work really well when used together.

This is because lean's emphasis on reducing waste supports Six Sigma's focus on quality, thereby eliminating most opportunities to have defects. By the same vein, Six Sigma's value for the highest quality supports lean's goals on process efficiency, as consistency plus the absence of reworks leads to faster cycle times.

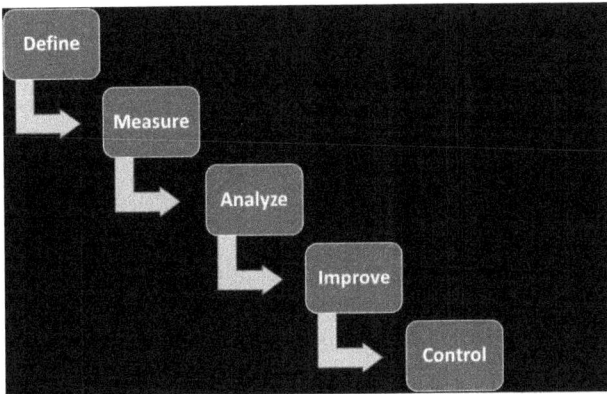

The DMAIC Roadmap

Figure 11. *The problem-solving process of Six Sigma*

Earlier, we mentioned that Six Sigma identifies and eliminates wastes by using the DMAIC method. This is a five-step framework that aims to reorganize current work processes such that every task produces a consistent output. Here's how a Six Sigma project typically starts:

• **Define**: This stage explores particular problems that can be worked on plus the objectives behind solving these problems. The following items are outlined and discussed in detail:

- Problem statement and objectives

- Project scope

- Required resources plus timeline

- Projected benefits

• **Measure**: This is the data-gathering stage. The different variables involved in work processes are measured, and data is collected afterwards. From here, baselines or standards are set. This will be used to compare performance metrics across time periods. The capability of the newer processes will then be measured accordingly.

• **Analyze**: This is where root-cause analysis takes place. The goal is to identify all the root causes of a particular defect in the product or in the process. This will help determine an appropriate solution that really addresses the problem.

• **Improve**: Once the root causes of the problems have been identified, the next step is to come up with solutions for improvement. This involves the conceptualization and testing of various solutions through experiments and simulation studies. Prototypes and beta versions are made to determine how feasible they are for short-term and long-term implementation.

• **Control**: After testing various solutions, their performances are documented in detail. Control systems are then installed to record their rates of improvement. Additionally, response plans are waiting should there be a failure in a particular solution.

Control charts show how each solution performs relative to the others. The process undergoes standardization, while the development of work instructions ensures that the process maintains consistency. The actual benefits of the project are then compared to its initial projected benefits. Ultimately, this stage is all about maintaining process gains.

While lean alone or Six Sigma alone can improve business workflows, an integrated approach like Lean Six Sigma may be better at helping you reap the full benefits of having a zero-waste process.

The lean portion usually takes care of removing wastes, while Six Sigma further polishes it by minimizing the variations of processes. It's all about continuously improving the organization's performance by eliminating errors that delay the most important tasks in the value stream.

Who Will Gain from Lean Six Sigma?

When applied correctly, Lean Six Sigma will clean up the messes of your business' entire workflow. As a result, it creates a bigger infrastructure for various processes, thereby allowing tasks to move without getting caught up in a bottleneck.

Of course, the benefits of Lean Six Sigma aren't limited to the company's owners or managers. It also extends to the following groups:

• **Employees**: When cultural resistance has been overcome, employees become more accepting of the upcoming company changes. As a result of the renewed openness to change, Lean Six Sigma is bound to improve your employees' job performance.

Consequently, the goal for continuous improvement means that they'll constantly undergo training to keep their skills and knowledge updated. This can be fulfilling even on a personal level.

• **Customers**: When efficiency and defect reduction are combined, customers will always get products that really improve their lives.

• **Suppliers**: Variations and defects usually come from raw materials. Lean Six Sigma can help suppliers determine the root cause of these variations and work on eliminating their occurrences in the future. This lowers the overall costs of creating the materials.

• **Stockholders**: Consistency in materials, products, and workflows can significantly reduce the costs needed for reworks, capitals, storage capacities, and staffing.

Just like lean, Six Sigma and Lean Six Sigma are effective tools in minimizing the need for additional resources. It operates on the premise that high standards can be achieved by maintaining the consistency of products and processes. Diversity is typically celebrated, but in Six Sigma, the lower the variation, the better.

Takeaway:

• Lean and Six Sigma are systems that aim to improve workflow through waste elimination and variation reduction. Though different in their approach, they share the same ultimate goal of making processes efficient and producing the best products for their customers. Lean Six Sigma integrates these two systems to optimize every facet of the value stream.

- The DMAIC roadmap is what fuels the Six Sigma problem-solving process. It seeks to define a problem and works on it until a maintainable solution with good improvement potential has been found.

- Managers and company owners aren't the only ones who are going to benefit from Lean Six Sigma. Other groups that will get to experience its good effects include employees, customers, suppliers, and stockholders.

Chapter 5:

The Kanban System for Backlog Reduction

"How does a project get to be a year late? One day at a time."

—Frederick Brooks

Most of us have gotten stressed at one point because of delayed projects. Such issues are usually blamed on a person's lack of time management skills. While that is definitely a logical cause of delays, sometimes the inability to manage time isn't really the problem. It's more of the inability to minimize works in progress (WIPs).

This is similar when you have multiple tabs open all at once. Even if you actually know the order in which to get to them, the right sequence will eventually be lost on you. This is how workplace wastes usually start out. When employees are always switching tasks, they never stay at one task long enough to actually progress to the next step.

As a result, most of them will always be "busy", yet they are rarely every productive. In such cases, applying the Kanban system may just be what you need to eliminate employee unproductivity and backlogs once and for all.

Kanban: The Original Scheduling System for Lean Manufacturing

Kanban means "card" or "signboard" in Japanese. It first came into existence as the scheduling system used by the Toyota Production System to properly execute their just-in-time product workflows.

Because the production line relies on customer demand, they needed a system that could help them visualize the entire flow across the value stream. Hence, they used actual cards to signify which tasks are already done, and which ones are still awaiting completion. This ensured that no one was doing too much at any one point.

The Core Principles of Kanban

Kanban's primary focus is to ensure that everyone's tasks are accomplished on schedule and that no backlogs will cause a significant impediment in the workflow. The following principles highlight how Kanban succeeds as a lean tool:

- **Workflow Visualization**

If you really want to see how every checkpoint in the value stream is related with each other, a Kanban board will show you how tasks move between stages. By pulling and moving cards from the "In Progress" column to the "Finished" column, employees can find it a lot easier to recognize which tasks should be prioritized, and which should already be delivered.

This is usually done using an actual board that's subdivided into columns, with tasks written on cards. It can also be a digital version, using a customized program or app.

- **WIP Reduction**

As mentioned in Chapter 1, context switching is usually one of the biggest sources of waste.

When an employee or a whole team's focus shifts at the middle of their current tasks, it typically harms the whole workflow. Kanban reduces the WIPs allowed in every stage so employees can work on tasks only when the Kanban board says they're free to do so.

- **Flow Management**

Kanban is mainly fueled by its goal of making workflows as smooth and as trouble-free as possible. By revealing the whole process in visual form, it becomes easier for managers to see how the process can be sped up in a sustainable manner.

Instead of keeping employees busy, Kanban allows the manager's focus to shift to the workflow and figure out how tasks can move through the value stream at a faster rate.

- **Feedback Loops**

Regular updates are also scheduled to keep everyone in the loop. These short meetings are generally done in front of the Kanban board to let everyone know what their tasks are, together with those tasks' current status.

Feedback loops put everyone in the same page. Additionally, operations reviews, service reviews, and risk reviews are also conducted at regular intervals to further encourage process improvement.

Integrating Kanban into the Workplace

A Kanban board that is filled with employees' necessary tasks is one of the simplest solutions you can apply if you want to know where your bottlenecks usually lie. The effort to do this change is also simple enough to overcome any resistance. Overall, Kanban simplifies the route your tasks are going to take.

Kanban boards usually come in 3 to 5 columns. The 3-columned ones are usually labeled with "Requested", "In Progress", and "Finished". The 5-columned ones have the "In Progress" column subdivided into three parts: "Working", "Waiting", and "Review". Depending on what your organization needs, your Kanban board can be as simple or as complex as you need it to be.

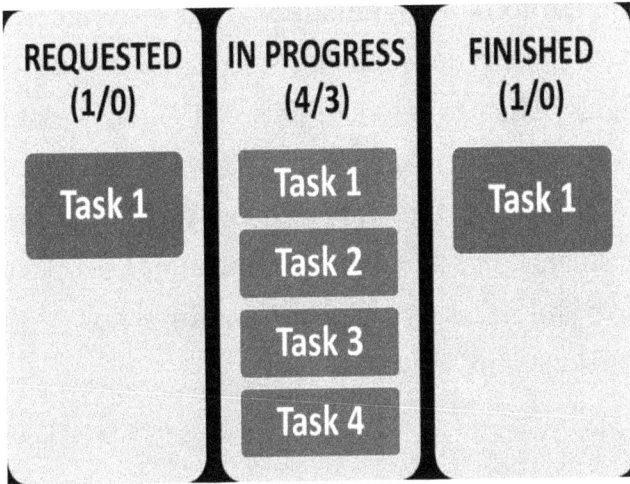

Figure 12. *A 3-column Kanban board showing a bottleneck at the "In Progress" stage*

Since Kanban is a highly visual system, it immediately reveals what's delaying the entire work process. In Figure 12, we can see that Column 2 has more tasks than what is recommended. Hence, managers and employees can work together to find ways on how these cases can be minimized — especially when it's happening too often.

Fortunately, Kanban is flexible and versatile enough to be integrated into your current work system without causing a company culture shock. The changes can be small enough that it wouldn't even take extreme efforts to sustain. It may not be the cure-all for your workflow problems, but it can at least encourage people to take the necessary steps to improve how tasks are done and delivered.

Takeaway:

• Kanban, a Japanese term which means "card" or "signboard", was first used as a tool in TPS to help Toyota employees visualize the tasks that should flow down the production line.

• Kanban is all about getting things done and removing things from your current workload. Its tactic for doing so is by limiting WIPs as much as possible so no one gets stuck at a particular checkpoint. This also ensures that employees devote their attention only to what's on their plate, instead of constantly switching to other tasks.

Chapter 6:

The 5S Process for Workspace Organization

"A clean warehouse means employees can move around more quickly and get things done easier. It's just common sense."

—Lee House

Lean Six Sigma and Kanban are tools that improve work process efficiency by eliminating wastes and applying necessary changes to the current value stream. Both of them tend to be more mental in nature — meaning, the changes usually come from a gradual shift in people's understanding of company-specific workflows. Given that, can wastes be eliminated in ways other than changing the mindset of the whole workforce?

Workspaces and Process Efficiency

Apparently, applying physical changes to your current office setup can also improve your workflow significantly. We're not just talking

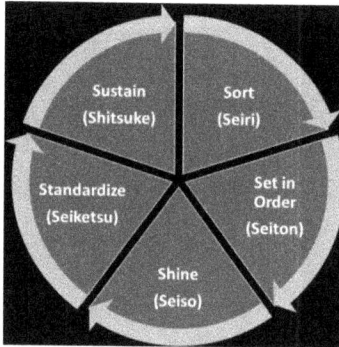

about eliminating transport and motion wastes, in which layouts are modified to simplify the movement between processes. We're also talking about putting everything in their rightful place.

Figure 13. *The 5S cycle for systematic neatness in the workplace*

This is exactly what the 5S process is for. Each S in the cycle aims to organize workspaces such that all tasks can be performed safely and efficiently. It operates on the idea that if the workplace is kept clean and things are where they should be, it will be easier for employees to accomplish their tasks without wasting their time on non-value adding steps or exposing themselves to safety hazards.

Like Kanban, just-in-time, and jidoka, 5S is a concept that started out as a tool at the Toyota production floor. In fact, 5S is regarded as a foundational component of the Toyota Production System because it helped keep the workplace neat and highly organized. This methodology was put in place because they knew how difficult it was to produce consistent results when a place is utterly messy.

Mistakes, delays, and accidents are probably not immediately blamed on all the clutter in the workplace. However, if you really think about it, all the mess usually prevents people from focusing on their jobs. Consequently, this only impedes the flow and it's only a matter of time before everyone gets stuck on the same spot.

Hence, to ensure the functionality of a workspace, the 5S can be used as a standard for maintaining order and structure. The terms were originally in Japanese, but close equivalents are used for the English translation. Here's what they stand for:

- **Sort (Seiri / Tidiness)**

The first stage involves the examination of all the tools and equipment that are currently present in the area. The goal is to determine which of them should stay and which of them should be removed to free up some space. At the end of this process, only the necessary tools should be left behind. Thus, it's worth asking:

- What's the purpose of this particular item?

- Who's using it?

- When was the last time it was used?

- How often do people use it?

- Is it really a necessity in this workspace?

The best people to ask regarding the items' value would be the people who are actually working in that area. For items that have been tagged as "unnecessary", these may be given away to another department, recycled, sold, thrown away, or put into the storage.

• **Set in Order (Seiton / Orderliness)**

Now that you've set which tools or equipment will remain, you can now proceed to organizing items based on what reduces motion wastes the most. The key is to remember the statement, "A place for everything; everything in its place."

This means that things shouldn't just be grouped together in a logical manner, but they should also be placed in a logical location. For instance, if an item is used frequently, it should be located in a place where it's easy to pull out.

• **Shine (Seiso / Cleanliness)**

Of course, keeping an area clean and organized requires work. Although it sounds very trivial, general cleaning is important enough to actually be involved as a crucial step in this process.

This stage emphasizes the regular cleaning of work areas, which includes putting items in their storage, sweeping, mopping, wiping, etc. This also includes regular equipment maintenance. Cleanliness ensures that problems don't go hidden by clutter, while maintenance prolongs the lifespan of your tools and equipment.

• **Standardize(Seiketsu/Standardizat ion)**

In order to know which strategies are really working for you, detailed documentation must be conducted. This helps you establish standards that serve as an instant reference for how 5S can be maintained in your company.

Oftentimes the workplace instantly transforms when you've completed the first three stages of 5S. Making the changes permanent is usually the next challenge. To turn the new habits into a lifestyle, standards must be put in place. These can be in the form of setting schedules or assigning routines. Standards ensure that all your efforts towards order will not go to waste.

• **Sustain (Shitsuke / Discipline)**

When the cleanup process has finally been standardized, you must then do the necessary work to maintain your new routines and update them as the situation deems fit. This final stage is all about keeping 5S going with the help of the entire workforce — from the managers to the employees.

The goal is to make 5S a long-term commitment, and not just a short-term solution for workflow efficiency. When people are disciplined enough to stick with 5S, it usually yields remarkable improvements.

Although 5S is relatively budget-friendly, its full effectivity still relies on your available resources. At the very least, it will involve expenses during the cleaning process. Additionally, you will need to train your employees regularly and acquire supplies such as labeling, shelving, floor markings, etc. to sustain the new practice.

In theory, the 5S methodology is very similar to a general house cleaning. In the workplace, however, there is this added consideration of whether item placements help in any way with movement and employee convenience. The general consensus is, the more convenient it is for everyone to get what they really need, the better.

Of course, starting the whole process can be daunting at first, especially if your workspaces haven't been neat for quite some time. Fortunately, implementing 5S can start small, and you only need to assign a few individuals — or one team at a time — to begin the process. A training module is highly recommended to show the full benefits of 5S over the long term.

Ultimately, the 5S methodology believes that a clean workspace is a productive workspace. If people never have to waste time looking for things ever again, then a general cleanup is indeed a great investment.

Takeaway:

The 5S stands for sort (seiri), set in order (seiton), shine (seiso), standardize (seiketsu), and sustain (shitsuke). This methodology encourages everyone in the workplace to keep a neat environment to boost productivity and enhance safety.

Conclusion: Greatness is Possible in the Absence of Wastes

"To be competitive, we have to look for every opportunity to improve efficiencies and productivity while increasing quality. Lean manufacturing principles have improved every aspect of our processes."

—Cynthia Fanning

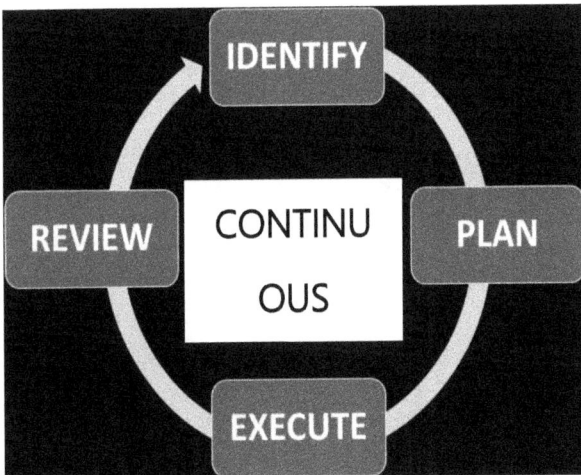

Figure 14. *How lean is implemented using the continuous improvement cycle*

Wastes are the main adversaries of long-term productivity and cost-effectiveness in any organization. This is where lean thinking comes in. Lean is a methodology that aims to eliminate wastes at every part of the value stream. So far, lean has identified 8 Deadly Wastes, which can be remembered by the acronym DOWNTIME. It stands for:

- **Defects**

- **Overproduction**

- **Waiting**

- **Non-utilized Talent**

- **Transport**

- **Inventory**

- **Motion**

- **Excess Processing**

In the lean context, wastes are defined as anything that doesn't add value to the company's end product. This refers to extra efforts that don't make a particular item any more valuable to its end user. Hence, additional labor or materials spent on fixing defects is considered waste.

Eliminating these wastes involves a thorough assessment of your work processes plus the application of various lean tools. Some of the lean methodologies that we discussed in this book include:

• **Just-in-Time (JIT)**: A set-up where every component can be pulled conveniently when there is customer demand. Instead of assembling products way ahead of time, hoping that the market wants it, just-in-time kickstarts a process only when customers ask for the product themselves.

Since efficiency is already a part of the mix, the company can deliver the product "just in time" even if they didn't have one assembled in the storage.

• **Jidoka**: Also known as "automation with a human touch", it involves the management of multiple machines that detect and prevent defects. This is because a machine automatically stops its operations when the process is completed or when a defective item has been produced. This prevents the whole system from producing any more defective materials, thereby saving time and costs.

• **Lean Six Sigma**: Lean and Six Sigma are methodologies that both specialize in waste elimination, they just have different approaches for doing so. While lean focuses on creating a smoother workflow, Six Sigma aims for production that is 99.99996% error-free.

Combined, Lean Six Sigma is a great tool for addressing both workflow quality and product perfection.

• **Kanban**: Kanban is a highly visual scheduling system used at the Toyota production floor. It consists of task cards that are pulled and transferred according to where they are in the value stream.

Because it's visual, it makes it a lot easier to detect where the process bottlenecks usually are. Kanban is one of the easiest changes that you can apply when you are thinking of shifting to lean, as it doesn't require a high-degree of commitment to maintain.

• **The 5S Process**: Neatness and cleanliness are the forefronts of the 5S methodology. It operates on the idea that if everything is where they should be, it's bound to save on a lot of costs, time, and resources.

True enough, a lot of waste comes from a simple inconvenience in workspace layout and item placements. 5S solves this right at the core and provides an environment that allows everyone to work without worrying where things are supposed to be.

It can be quite overwhelming to apply the lean tools that you've learned all at once. Surely, your intentions for a better, more efficient workflow may be met with resistance if you attempt to apply massive changes that are the total opposite of your current systems. However, by taking little steps and laying out its benefits in a clear manner, it will be easier for you to get everyone on board.

Wastes can be insidious, and you may not even realize how much your current processes are plagued with them. But if you decide to start small now, you'll definitely see huge benefits if you stick with it for at least a few months.

Lean concepts are generally best applied on a personal level first. When you're managing people that are already lean within themselves, it will become so much easier to apply it as a company-wide culture. And, in becoming a lean company, you can then put yourself out there and work with other lean companies to build a lean enterprise.

Thank you

Before you go, I just wanted to say thank you for purchasing my book.

You could have picked from dozens of other books on the same topic but you took a chance and chose this one.

So, a HUGE thanks to you for getting this book and for reading all the way to the end.

Now I wanted to ask you for a small favor. ***Could you please consider posting a review on the platform? Reviews are one of the easiest ways to support the work of independent authors.***

This feedback will help me continue to write the type of books that will help you get the results you want. So if you enjoyed it, please let me know!

Resources Page

5S Today. (n.d.). What is 5S? Retrieved November 9, 2019, from https://www.5stoday.com/what-is-5s/

American Society for Quality. (n.d.). What is lean? Retrieved November 5, 2019, from https://asq.org/quality-resources/lean

APB Consultant. (2017, September 7). Lean enterprise. Retrieved November 9, 2019, from http://isoconsultantpune.com/lean-enterprise/

Aslinger, G. (2014, November 17). Lean six sigma for beginners. Retrieved November 9, 2019, from https://www.processexcellencenetwork.com/lean-six-sigma-business-performance/articles/continuous-improvement-with-lean-six-sigma-for-beg

Do, D. (2017, August 5). The five principles of lean. Retrieved November 7, 2019, from https://theleanway.net/The-Five-Principles-of-Lean

EnPower Group. (n.d.). Lean enterprise management. Retrieved November 4, 2019, from http://enpowergroup.com/lean-enterprise/

GoLeanSixSigma. (n.d.). DMAIC: The 5 phases of lean six sigma. Retrieved November 9, 2019, from https://goleansixsigma.com/dmaic-five-basic-phases-of-lean-six-sigma/

Ingram, D. (2017, November 21). Key Issues for the Implementation of a Lean Manufacturing System. Retrieved November 9, 2019, from https://smallbusiness.chron.com/key-issues-implementation-lean-manufacturing-system-75390.html

Investopedia. (2019, October 6). Lean startup. Retrieved November 5, 2019, from https://www.investopedia.com/terms/l/lean-startup.asp

Jansson, K. (2017, May 2). "Lean thinking" and the 5 principles of lean manufacturing. Retrieved November 4, 2019, from https://blog.kainexus.com/improvement-disciplines/lean/lean-thinking-and-the-5-principles-of-lean-manufacturing

Johnson, J. (2019, July 30). Lean vs. six sigma: What's the difference & use cases. Retrieved November 9, 2019, from https://tallyfy.com/lean-vs-six-sigma/

Kanbanize. (n.d.). Kanban explained for beginners. Retrieved November 9, 2019, from https://kanbanize.com/kanban-resources/getting-started/what-is-kanban/

Lean Manufacturing Junction. (2019, October 14). Benefits of lean manufacturing: What can it do for your company? Retrieved November 9, 2019, from https://www.lean-manufacturing-junction.com/benefits-of-lean/

LeanKit. (2018, October 8). Lean, kanban, and how they work together. Retrieved November 9, 2019, from https://leankit.com/learn/lean/lean-kanban/

Martin, J. R. (n.d.). Lean company vs. lean enterprise. Retrieved November 5, 2019, from https://maaw.info/ArticleSummaries/ArtSum WomackAndJones94.htm

McArdle, C. (2017, December 27). 10 benefits of applying a lean methodology. Retrieved November 9, 2019, from https://www.kaizenkulture.com/blog/10-benefits-of-applying-a-lean-methodology

Proqis. (n.d.). An introduction to the Toyota production system and principles. Retrieved November 6, 2019, from http://insights.btoes.com/lean-resources/toyota-production-system-principles-introduction-to-tps

Rastogi, A. (n.d.). A brief introduction to lean, six sigma, and lean six sigma. Retrieved November 9, 2019, from https://www.greycampus.com/blog/quality-management/a-brief-introduction-to-lean-and-six-sigma-and-lean-six-sigma

Rever Team. (2019, May 16). Lean thinking: Principles to scale effectively. Retrieved November 5, 2019, from https://reverscore.com/lean-thinking/

Rodriguez, T. S. (2018, November 3). LEAN production: The method that made Toyota the most valuable car brand in the world. Retrieved November 6, 2019, from https://medium.com/drill/lean-production-the-method-that-made-toyota-the-most-valuable-car-brand-in-the-world-13279db0b224

Terry, J. (2019, September 10). Lean thinking: The foundation of lean practice. Retrieved November 5, 2019, from https://www.planview.com/resources/articles/lean-thinking-lean-practice/

Terry, J. (2019, November 6). What is kanban? Retrieved November 9, 2019, from https://www.planview.com/resources/articles/what-is-kanban/

The Lean Startup. (n.d.). The lean startup principles. Retrieved November 5, 2019, from http://theleanstartup.com/principles

Universal Class. (n.d.). Lean thinking concepts. Retrieved November 5, 2019, from https://www.universalclass.com/articles/business/lean-thinking-concepts.htm

Wastradowski, M. (n.d.). What is 5S? Retrieved November 9, 2019, from https://www.graphicproducts.com/articles/what-is-5s/

Womack, J. P., & Jones, D. T. (2014, August 1). From lean production to the lean enterprise. Retrieved November 4, 2019, from https://hbr.org/1994/03/from-lean-production-to-the-lean-enterprise